All Saints
All Souls
and Halloween

A WORLD OF HOLIDAYS

All Saints
All Souls
and Halloween

Catherine Chambers

RSVP

RAINTREE
STECK-VAUGHN
P U B L I S H E R S
The Steck-Vaughn Company

Austin, Texas

Published by Raintree Steck-Vaughn Publishers,
an imprint of Steck-Vaughn Company

Library of Congress Cataloging-in-Publication Data

Chambers, Catherine.
    All Saints, All Souls, and Halloween / Catherine Chambers.
       p.   cm. — (A world of holidays)
    Includes bibliographical references and index.
    Summary: Examines the traditions and celebrations occurring around the world on Halloween, All Saints' Day, and All Souls' Day, festival days at the end of October and beginning of November that bring fire and mystery to the onset of winter.
    ISBN 0-8172-4606-1
    1. Halloween—Juvenile literature.   2. All Saints' Day—Juvenile literature.   3. All Souls' Day—Juvenile literature.
    [1. Halloween.   2. All Saints' Day.   3. All Souls' Day]
    I. Title. II. Series.
GT4965.C47   1997
394.2'646—dc20   96-34334
                           CIP
                           AC

Printed in Spain
Bound in the United States
1 2 3 4 5 6 7 8 9 0 99 98 97 96

ACKNOWLEDGMENTS

Editor: Su Swallow, Pam Wells
Design: Neil Sayer
Production: Jenny Mulvanny

For permission to reproduce copyright material, the author and publishers gratefully acknowledge the following:

Title page Emma Lee/Life File
page 5 Robert Harding Picture Library page 6 Edward Parker/Hutchison Library page 7 (top left) Last Resort (bottom right) Hutchison Library page 8 David Reed/Panos Pictures page 9 (top) Ronald Sheridan/Ancient Art and Architecture Collection (bottom) Hutchison Library page 10 (top) Robert Francis/Hutchison Library (bottom) Mike Potter/Life File page 11 Sally-Anne Fison/Life File page 12 (top) Jeremy Hartley/Panos Pictures (bottom) David Cumming/Eye Ubiquitous page 13 Billie Cook/Life File page 14 (top) Crispin Hughes/Panos Pictures (bottom) Trevor Page/Hutchison Library page 15 (top) James Davis Travel Photography (bottom) Robert Francis/Hutchison Library page 16 Circa Photo Library/John Smith page 17 (top) Ancient Art and Architecture Collection (bottom) James Davis Travel Photography page 18 Collections/Brian Shuel page 19 (top) Emma Lee/Life File (bottom) Gregory Wrona/Panos Pictures page 20 Simon Arnold/Eye Ubiquitous page 21 (top) Robert Frerck/Robert Harding Picture Library (bottom) Andy Purcell/Bruce Coleman Limited page 22 (top) Robert Frerck/Robert Harding Picture Library (bottom) Robert Francis/Hutchison Library page 23 Alan Towse Photography page 24 George McCarthy/Bruce Coleman Limited page 25 (top) Angela Maynard/Life File (bottom) Robert Harding Picture Library page 26 Frank Lane Picture Agency page 27 Mary Evans Picture Library page 28 Alan Towse Photography page 29 Alan Towse Photography

 Contents

 Spirits, Saints, and the Sun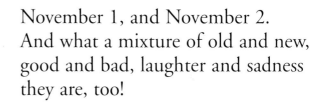

It is the end of autumn. As winter darkness approaches, the souls of the dead and the spirits of kind saints are all remembered with three festivals, or holidays.

WHEN CAN WE CELEBRATE?

Halloween, All Saints' Day, and All Souls' Day bring fire and mystery to the beginning of winter. These three days are all holidays. They are celebrated on October 31, November 1, and November 2. And what a mixture of old and new, good and bad, laughter and sadness they are, too!

In the chilly mists of autumn, people held festivals to keep spirits happy.

CHRISTIANS JOIN IN!

The Christian religion began about 2,000 years ago. Christians follow the teachings of Jesus Christ. But long ago, many Christians still wanted to keep their old religious festivals. So the early Church just added their own to the old ones. Their celebrations for the spirits of saints and the souls of the dead fit in well at this time of the year.

During All Saints' Day, glowing fires welcomed home the spirits of the dead.

BEGINNINGS

Early November in Europe is chilly and misty. In fact, it is really spooky. Long ago, at this time of year, religious people remembered the spirits. The good spirits were kept happy with food and warm fires. But the bad ones were chased away.

Another religious custom was in honor of the sun. Winter can be a dark time, and in those days only lamps and firelight brightened the long nights. It seemed as if the sun would never shine brightly again. So huge fires were lit to give the sun strength through the long winter.

All Saints' Day is a time for remembering the spirits of saints. This is Saint Cecilia, the patron saint of music.

❤ The Souls of the Dead ❤

People from all over the world believe that the dead have souls that live on. Their spirits can be very powerful, perhaps especially at Halloween and All Souls!

Spirit religions are important in Africa and the Americas. Spiritual healers use special medicines and the power of the spirits to cure the sick.

FAMILY SPIRITS

Before the Christian religion burst into northern Africa and Europe, most people believed in many gods, often with one chief god in charge. They also believed in the power of spirits, both good and bad.

Halloween was a very old Anglo-Saxon and Celtic spirit festival, or holidays, and the beginning of the Celtic New Year.

The Celtic celebration was known as Samhain in those days. Samhain was the Celtic Lord of the Dead. At the festival each family remembered all its ancestors' spirits. The family made new links with them for the year ahead to keep the souls happy.

Samhain judged all the dead souls during the holiday. People offered gifts to him. Then he might judge the spirits kindly and let them go home for the night.

But the celebration of Samhain was a night of turmoil, too. Ghosts and demons rose from the dead and ran around making mischief!

Some Celtic traditions—and some Celtic jewelery—have survived to today.

SPIRITS OF THE WORLD

Christians believe in spirits, too. They believe in life after death. So it was not difficult for the early Church to accept a holiday for dead souls.

When people from Europe moved to America about 500 years ago, they took Halloween customs with them. African slaves in America added their own spirit traditions to the Celtic and Christian ones. What a rich mixture!

In Brazil, Umbanda grew out of the belief in the spirits held by African slaves.

✔ It's Halloween! ✔

It's October 31. The spirits of the dead are whirling around in a frenzy! They are trying to find their way home. Witches and demons in scary costumes are on the loose. Watch out!

PRAYERS FOR SOULS

The name *Halloween* was given to this holiday by the early Roman Catholic Church. It means "All Hallows' Eve," the night before All Saints' Day.

Although Halloween is an old holiday, it's still very much alive. In

A woman leaves flowers at a grave in a small Italian town.

Europe and South America, many people celebrate Halloween with Christian customs.

In the past, people visited the graves of their ancestors. There, they could think about them and say prayers for them. Today, many people still visit graves with candles and greetings cards.

MODERN MISCHIEF

The Celts kept the spirits happy with fires, feasts, dancing, and gifts. Some people wore ghostly masks. They hoped to trick naughty spirits into thinking that they were spirits,

In a Russian church, a candle is lit for a loved soul.

too. The people in disguise then led the wicked demons to the edge of the village. Here, they could do no evil deeds or harm.

Today, Halloween is still a special night in America. Young and old alike go out in spooky clothes and threatening masks. Some dress as witches or demons. But others dress as cartoon characters, as princesses, or even as astronauts if they like. Anything goes!

Two young girls in Texas are out to scare their friends in spooky skeleton costumes. They're going trick or treating. (See pages 22–23.)

❦A Host of Saints❦

At least one Christian saint is remembered on each day of the year. And on November 1, there is a special celebration for all the saints. But what makes a saint?

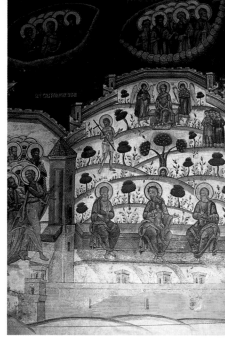

A host of saints in a church in Romania.

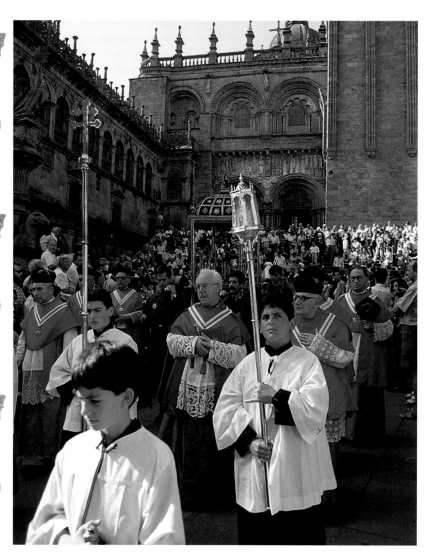

It is Saint James' Day in the city of Santiago de Compostela in Spain. The bones of Saint James lie in the church there.

A LONG LIST

Saints became part of the Roman Catholic and Orthodox Churches very early on. At first, all Christians were thought to be saints. But about 100 years later, only people who died for their belief in Jesus Christ became saints. Then the list grew to include Christians who had led good lives. Now there are thousands of them!

Some are the twelve teachers chosen by Jesus Christ. Others are those who helped the sick and the poor. There are lots of special ones, too.

Some are the national saints for countries where most people are Christian. For example, Saint James is the saint for Spain. Other saints are special to different kinds of workers, such as fishers and musicians—or even motorists.

SAINTLY HELP

For many Christians, saints are like real, living people. A believer can pray to a saint in times of trouble. If his or her life changes for the better, it could be because a saint helped the believer. If someone wants to talk to God, it is sometimes easier to pray to a saint first. There are lots of festivals for saints. In southern Europe and South America, saints' days are celebrated in a very big way with parades, dancing, and fireworks.

Dancing is one of the ways of celebrating saints' days. A maypole is used especially on Saint John's Day here in Spain, and in Portugal, too.

ꙮ All Saints' Day ꙮ

After the spirits and witches of Halloween comes a very different holiday. The first day of November is a day for celebrating all the saints— even those who are not born yet!

A service for the saints in the African countryside.

A statue of St. Francis of Assisi is paraded through the streets on All Saints' Day.

SAINTLY STATUES

All Saints' Day is a public holiday in many Roman Catholic countries. There are bells and church services. Statues of the saints are paraded through the streets. But how did this all begin?

THE CHURCH MAKES CHANGES

The early Church wasn't very happy that Christians kept customs linked with witches and bad spirits. But the old traditions would not die. So about 1,300 years ago, the Church began to celebrate all the saints instead.

The first celebration took place when Christian leaders changed the Pantheon of Rome into a church. The Pantheon was a temple full of statues of the old Roman gods. The Church wanted to get rid of the

14

This huge church in Rome now remembers all the saints that died for their faith. But it was once known as the Pantheon, a temple for all the Roman gods.

temple. But they wanted to give people something in its place. So they made it into a church for all the saints who had died for their faith.

Then about 200 years later, the Pope, the leader of the Roman Catholic Church, decided to hold a Festival of All Saints at the beginning of November. The Pope knew that early November was when the biggest festivals for ancient religions took place in northern Europe.

The idea was a clever one. It let people celebrate their old festivals. But it gave them a new Christian one, too.

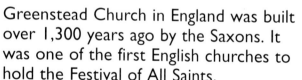

Greenstead Church in England was built over 1,300 years ago by the Saxons. It was one of the first English churches to hold the Festival of All Saints.

All Souls' Day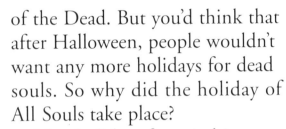

The spirits have settled, and the witches have flown. Saints in all their glory have been praised. On November 2, the souls of the dead must be properly honored. Then, they too can rest.

PRAYERS FOR THE DEAD

In many churches around the world, people gather to pray for the dead on All Souls' Day. The Roman Catholic Church holds three full services, or masses, to give peace to their souls. In Mexico, the festival is very special. It is known as the Day of the Dead. But you'd think that after Halloween, people wouldn't want any more holidays for dead souls. So why did the holiday of All Souls take place?

After holidays for mischievous spirits and good saints, ordinary souls really needed one of their own. So nearly 1,000 years after the birth of Jesus Christ, the Church gave them a holiday of their own. It began in Cluny, France. Over the next 300 years the holiday spread to southern and eastern Europe and to the British Isles.

THE CRIES OF LOST SOULS

Some people believe that the festival began with a story of a Christian man who made a holy journey all the way to Jerusalem. This was the city where Jesus Christ had died.

On his return, the ship broke up

A Roman Catholic mass is held for the souls of the dead so that they can rest in peace.

in a stormy sea. The Christian was tossed onto an island. There he met a man who said he could hear the cries of dead souls. They were coming from a crack that went deep into burning rock. The Christian traveled on to the church at Cluny. There, he told his story to the head monk, or abbot, who then made November 2 a day to pray for all dead souls, to give them peace.

▲ When a Christian was shipwrecked on his way home from Jerusalem, he was told about the cries of dead souls.

◄ The French abbey church of Cluny is where the holiday of All Souls began.

Furious Fires and Glowing Lights

In November, the Celts lit bonfires to keep the sun burning through the winter. Now, pumpkin lanterns ward off bad spirits. The candles shine for the souls of the dead.

BUILD A BONFIRE!

There's nothing like the smell of an autumn bonfire! Long ago at this time, bonfire ashes were spread over farmland to help crops grow. This custom fit in well with the fires that warmed the weak winter sun. The Catholic Church did not mind keeping these traditions at All Saints' Day.

But 500 years ago, some European Christians did not like Catholic customs. These Christians became a separate group called Protestants.

After November 5, 1605, English Protestants made an autumn fire celebration of their own. A Catholic, Guy Fawkes, was killed for trying to blow up the Protestant government. November 5 became a holiday. It was a day for burning great bonfires, with dummies of poor Guy Fawkes sitting on top.

In Great Britain, people still burn poor Guy Fawkes on bonfire night. The "Guy" is made from old clothes stuffed with newspaper or straw.

18

A LIGHT FOR EVERY SOUL

On Halloween, Irish people hollowed out turnips and set candles in them. They did this to turn away demons, who were afraid of the light. When the Irish came to America, they found that pumpkins made even better lanterns than turnips. That's why we have pumpkin lanterns today.

Cozy fires were lit at Halloween to warm chilly rooms. Then the souls of dead ancestors might come home.

The Christian Church added their own customs. On Halloween Eve, Catholics in Europe and South America carry candles to the graves of each of their loved ones.

▶ Does this pumpkin lantern give you a nice warm feeling? Or does it scare you to death?

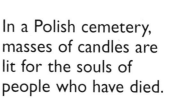

In a Polish cemetery, masses of candles are lit for the souls of people who have died.

19

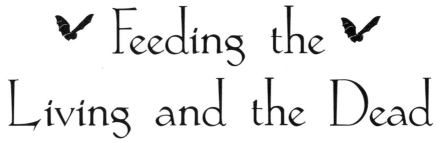

Feeding the Living and the Dead

This holiday is a time to eat "soul cakes" and party treats. But some people serve them to the souls of the dead.

COOKING FOR SOULS

Hundreds of years ago, people set out food and wine for their ancestors' spirits, to welcome them home. Later, the Church asked people to bake soul cakes instead. These were given to the poor, who then prayed for the givers' dead ancestors. After many years, boys went from house to house singing songs for the souls. They hoped to get soul cakes or even money in return.

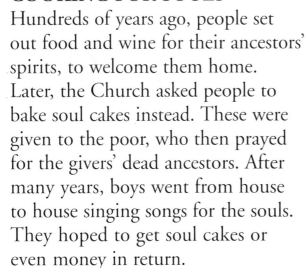

NO TALKING AT THE TABLE!

Have you ever heard of the "dumb (or silent) supper?" This is an eerie All Saints Day meal. No one speaks, not even a single whisper. It encourages the spirits to come to the table. The "silent supper" was brought to America by Africans.

THE MEXICAN DAY OF THE DEAD

In Mexico on November 1, women and young girls carry food to the cemeteries at midnight. They light candles and set up huge statues of skeletons. The men and young boys sing outside the cemetery gates. Inside, the food is offered first to the souls of the ancestors. Then, on November 2, as the Day of the Dead dawns, the food is shared among the people.

Soul cakes in the shape of graves are sold in Mexico City for the Day of the Dead.

On the Day of the Dead in Mexico, masses of flowers, glowing lights, and gifts show respect for the dead.

NUTCRACKER NIGHT

In Great Britain, people thought that the devil was a nut-gatherer. So at Halloween, people used nuts as magic charms. If a girl puts a sprig of the herb rosemary and a silver coin under her pillow on Halloween night, she will see her future husband in a dream!

Hazelnuts have special magical powers, especially during Halloween.

Ghastly Games

Trick or treating and bobbing for apples are two of the ghastly and ghostly games often played at Halloween.

TRICK OR TREAT? TRICK OR TREAT?

The United States is the place to be for Halloween fun. Over the last 200 years, the games have become brighter and richer. One of the greatest ways of having fun is to dress up in disguise. You can go to a Halloween party or parade in the street. But children get most fun out of trick or treating. The custom is a mixture of old Irish traditions and going around to houses singing for soul cakes.

"Eek!" A trick or treater will frighten the life out of you!

Scary skeletons and spooky spiders' webs decorate a house in New Baltimore, Michigan.

Dressed up as witches, clowns, or even Mickey Mouse, children wait till dark. Then they knock on neighbors' doors, shouting "Trick or treat?" If you don't want to get an unpleasant surprise, you'd better give them some sweet treats! Many children trick-or-treat with the special carton to collect money for UNICEF.

HAPPY APPLE BOBBING!

Apples are magic! Ancient Celts in Great Britain believed that heaven was filled with apple trees bursting with fruit. For the Romans, who invaded Britain, apples were a symbol of love. They were part of the autumn festival of Pomona. Bobbing for apples became a British and later a U.S. Halloween party tradition.

To play, fill a large bowl with water and float some apples in it. Ask players to take turns, putting their hands behind their backs. Then the players bend over the bowl and try to catch the apple stalks with their teeth. Then they can pull out the apples and eat them. No hands, please! It isn't as easy as it looks. And they're bound to get their faces wet!

These boys are hoping that the girls will drop their apples. No such luck!

❤Halloween Animals❤

Owls, bats, snails, and black cats. Are they lucky, or just plain spooky? They've been an important part of Halloween for hundreds of years.

FOUL OWLS

"Oh, no! Can you hear that owl hooting? Someone's going to die!" People used to think that owls swooped down to eat the souls of the dying. So if they heard an owl hooting, they were frightened. So what do you do to stop an owl from hooting? Try turning your pockets inside out, and you'll be all right!

BAD BLACK CATS?

Are black cats lucky or unlucky? There are lots of arguments about that! But a long time ago in Europe they had rather unpleasant connections with witches. In the United States, some people believed in the magic power of the black-cat bone. Certain bones had the power to make wishes come true—or even to make the bone owner invisible!

Today, this watchful owl is thought to be a wise, harmless bird.

In days gone by, this black cat would have been in hiding at Halloween!

SNAILS' TRAILS

Catch a snail on Halloween night and keep it in a flat dish. In the morning, you'll see the first letter of your sweetheart written in slime!

BEASTLY BATS?

Let's finish with nice animals—bats. In November at ancient Samhain holidays, bats used to swoop over blazing fires to guzzle all the—mosquitoes! Today during Halloween, the Atlanta Zoo opens the doors to its bat house. Would you dare to go in?

What secrets will this snail reveal?

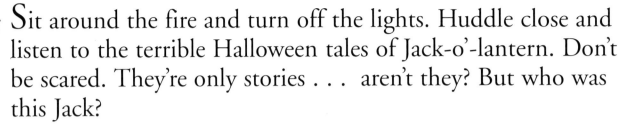 Scary Stories

Sit around the fire and turn off the lights. Huddle close and listen to the terrible Halloween tales of Jack-o'-lantern. Don't be scared. They're only stories . . . aren't they? But who was this Jack?

Jack was a lad who had no fear of the devil. He strolled to a crossroads at midnight to meet him. There, they made a deal. Jack said, "Look, you just let me have seven years full of all the fun I like. Then you can come and take me down to hell with you."

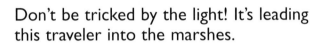

Don't be tricked by the light! It's leading this traveler into the marshes.

26

At night, marshland like this sometimes seems to glow with lights.

So Jack did just as he wanted for seven whole years. But the devil didn't forget about him. He knocked on Jack's door, and Jack let him in. "Come in, come in!" said he. "But before we set off for hell, just reach up above the door and get that old shoe for me—could you?"

The devil was happy to help. He stretched up his hand and—WHAM! Jack nailed the devil's hand to the wall. "I'll let you go," laughed Jack, "But you'll have to promise not to come for me anymore." The devil promised.

When Jack finally died, no one wanted his soul. Heaven refused him—so did hell. "Be off with you," snarled the devil as he threw a ball of fire at Jack.

So Jack just wanders, shining with his fiery glow. But he has his fun, too. Be careful at night. Don't follow his light. He likes to lead curious folks into a thick, sticky bog.

Jack-o'-lantern Halloween stories came from ancient Ireland and were taken to America many years ago. There, as with many customs, they were enriched by African traditions. Some stories tell the fate of people who follow the eerie dancing light that flickers over misty marshes. The light was known as Jack-o'-lantern.

27

❤ Let's Celebrate! ❤

Join in the Halloween fun! Try making some orange Halloween lanterns and a Halloween animal mobile.

MAKING A HALLOWEEN LANTERN

These are for a spooky, nighttime party outdoors. You should never light these (or anything else!) inside. When they're made, place them on stones or sand, well away from anything that can burn. As with fireworks, always keep a bucket of water handy.

Materials:
- large, soft oranges
- a knife—not too sharp
- safe scissors
- a night-light or small candle

Directions:
1. Cut the orange into two pieces. Make the top larger than the bottom.
2. Scoop out the insides and eat them, or make them into juice!
3. Cut a big hole in the top of the larger piece of orange. Then cut out eyes, a nose, and the top half of the mouth.
4. Cut out the mouth in the bottom half of the orange.
5. Put your night-light in the bottom half. Ask an adult to light it and put on the top half of the orange.

28

MAKING A HALLOWEEN MOBILE

Materials:

- colored cardboard—or you can paint white cardboard in different colors
- two sticks of the same length
- thread—such as fishing tackle or strong cotton
- safe scissors
- a thin knitting needle

Directions:

1. Cut your Halloween animal shapes. You can trace around pictures in a magazine or book as a guide.
2. Use the knitting needle to make a hole in the top of each animal.
3. Thread different lengths of fishing tackle or cotton through the holes. Tie the thread around the hole.
4. Crisscross the sticks and wind thread around and around the middle to tie the sticks together. Make a tight knot to finish. Tie a loop to hang up your mobile.
5. Now tie the animals to the sticks, wherever you want them. Move the animals up and down the sticks until the mobile balances.

Glossary

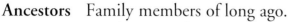

Ancestors Family members of long ago.
Ancient Describes something that is very old.
Celebrate To show that a certain day or event is special.
Celebrations Ways of celebrating a special day, such as parades or parties.
Demons Wicked spirits.
Saints Good people, thought to be especially holy after they have died.
Soul The human spirit—the soul leaves the body of a person at death.
Spirits Beings that you can't see—something like ghosts.
Temple A place of worship.
Tradition A custom, an old way of doing something.
UNICEF United Nations International Children's Emergency Fund.

Further Reading

Arndt, Ursula. *Witches, Pumpkins, and Grinning Ghosts: The Story of Halloween Symbols.* Houghton Mifflin (Clarion), 1981.

Flint, David. *Mexico.* Raintree Steck-Vaughn, 1993.

Fradin, Dennis B. *Halloween.* Enslow, 1990.

Jacobson, Karen. *Mexico.* Childrens, 1982.

Hopkins, Lee B. *Ragged Shadows: Poems of Halloween Night.* Little, 1993.

Leiner, Katherine. *Halloween.* S & S Childrens (Atheneum), 1993.

Index